Blind Spots
How Unhealthy Corridors Harm Communities
and How to Fix Them

**Urban Land
Institute**

Center for Sustainability
and Economic Performance

© 2019 by the Urban Land Institute

2001 L Street, NW | Suite 200 | Washington, DC 20036-4948

Recommended bibliographic listing: Zaccaro, Heather. *Blind Spots: How Unhealthy Corridors Harm Communities and How to Fix Them.* Washington, DC: Urban Land Institute, 2019.

ISBN: 978-0-87420-423-0

About the Urban Land Institute

The Urban Land Institute is a global, member-driven organization comprising more than 42,000 real estate and urban development professionals dedicated to advancing the Institute's mission of providing leadership in the responsible use of land and in creating and sustaining thriving communities worldwide.

ULI's interdisciplinary membership represents all aspects of the industry, including developers, property owners, investors, architects, urban planners, public officials, real estate brokers, appraisers, attorneys, engineers, financiers, and academics. Established in 1936, the Institute has a presence in the Americas, Europe, and Asia Pacific regions, with members in 80 countries.

The extraordinary impact that ULI makes on land use decision-making is based on its members sharing expertise on a variety of factors affecting the built environment, including urbanization, demographic and population changes, new economic drivers, technology advancements, and environmental concerns.

Peer-to-peer learning is achieved through the knowledge shared by members at thousands of convenings each year that reinforce ULI's position as a global authority on land use and real estate. In 2017 alone, more than 1,900 events were held in about 290 cities around the world.

Drawing on the work of its members, the Institute recognizes and shares best practices in urban design and development for the benefit of communities around the globe.

More information is available at uli.org. Follow ULI on Twitter, Facebook, LinkedIn, and Instagram.

About Smart Growth America

Smart Growth America is a national organization dedicated to researching, advocating for, and leading coalitions to bring better development to more communities nationwide. From providing more sidewalks to ensuring that more homes are built near public transportation or that productive farms remain a part of our communities, smart growth helps make sure people across the nation can live in great neighborhoods. Learn more at **www.smartgrowthamerica.org**.

Report Team

Primary Author

Heather Zaccaro
Program Manager, National
Complete Streets Coalition

Project Adviser

Sharon Roerty
Senior Program Officer
Robert Wood Johnson Foundation

Smart Growth America Project Staff

Emiko Atherton
Director, National Complete
Streets Coalition

Stephen Skilton
Economic Analyst

Jordan Chafetz
Economic Analyst

Stephen Lee Davis
Director, Communications

Michael Rodriguez
Director, Research

ULI Project Staff

Rachel MacCleery
Senior Vice President

Billy Grayson
Executive Director

Sara Hammerschmidt
Senior Director

James A. Mulligan
Senior Editor/Manuscript Editor

Brandon Weil
Art Director

Tom Cameron
Graphic Designer

Craig Chapman
Senior Director,
Publishing Operations

ULI Senior Executives

Ed Walter
Global Chief Executive Officer

Michael Terseck
Chief Financial Officer/Chief
Administrative Officer

Cheryl Cummins
Global Governance Officer

Lisette van Doorn
Chief Executive Officer,
ULI Europe

John Fitzgerald
Chief Executive Officer,
ULI Asia Pacific

Adam Smolyar
Chief Marketing and
Membership Officer

Steve Ridd
Executive Vice President,
Global Business Operations

Facing page: Aurora Avenue North in
Shoreline, Washington, a major arterial
that connects the suburb to Seattle,
underwent an infrastructure overhaul
that added sidewalks and bus lanes.

A corridor in Brooklyn, New York, incorporates many aspects of a healthy corridor, including trees, sidewalks, and well-marked bike lanes.

Contents

Appendixes

Available at **www.uli.org/healthycorridors**

Support for this research was provided by the
Robert Wood Johnson Foundation. The views
expressed in this publication do not necessarily
reflect the views of the Foundation.

Typical commercial corridors feature wide and numerous travel lanes with few considerations for pedestrians and bicyclists. (Boise, Idaho)

Introduction

Have you seen this street? It's a typical wide, high-speed road without safe places to walk or bike. Bus stops and crosswalks are few and far between—if there are any at all—and healthy food options are just as scarce. Seas of parking border both sides of the street.

You probably have one—or many—commercial corridors just like this in your own community, but you might not have given them much thought. Or possibly, your community may have been struggling to reimagine the function, aesthetics, and safety of a corridor like this for years.

Unhealthy corridors reside in our collective "blind spots"—they are neglected places that despite receiving growing attention have persisted and even proliferated. Although they are widely recognized as a problem on a community-by-community basis, until this report little was known about them as a whole.

Where are they most prevalent? How do they affect safety and commerce? Who is most affected? And why are unhealthy corridor conditions so widespread?

To answer these questions and others, the Urban Land Institute (ULI) and Smart Growth America (SGA) launched a joint research project to improve understanding of this problem and explore which policies and practices can help remake commercial corridors as places that promote health and well-being.

SIDEWALK ENDS

Above: A lack of safe infrastructure for pedestrians and bicyclists creates a barrier to physical activity. (Fayetteville, Arkansas)

Left: Insufficient crosswalks mean the most direct route for pedestrians is often unsafe. (Boise, Idaho)

Guy Hand

Why Unhealthy Corridors?

Unhealthy corridor conditions are all too familiar, and many communities around the country experience challenges in their commercial corridors. Traditionally, efforts to revamp commercial corridors have focused on economic redevelopment and luring new businesses, including large-format retailers, to underperforming corridors. Though economic development is a piece of the puzzle, the priority should be to help corridors better serve their communities and to transform them into safer, more vibrant, and healthier places.

Living and working conditions in communities have a profound impact on public health. Health is not just what happens in the doctor's office or the result of personal genetics. It is significantly influenced by the built and social environment—also known as the *social determinants of health,* which include housing conditions, transportation, education, and job opportunities.

Unhealthy corridor conditions pose barriers to healthy choices, including physical activity, and unhealthy corridors are not doing as good a job as they could in connecting workers to job opportunities. They serve to divide communities rather than tie them together. They are places to pass through, rather than linger. These unhealthy conditions are especially prevalent along corridors in low-income communities.

In the context of transportation networks, urban and suburban arterials are an essential but often overlooked and misunderstood link in a transportation chain, and they have outsized influence on their communities. They often struggle to balance the competing functions of moving cars quickly through a place and moving people to and from shops, restaurants, and other businesses safely.

The U.S. Department of Transportation defines arterial roads by their function, which is to move cars between highways and lower-capacity collector roads. But in many communities, arterials serve as the de facto main street. They host stores, restaurants, banks, and gyms. They link neighborhoods with each other and residents with job opportunities.

And unfortunately, despite playing these roles, all too often they are designed and operated in ways that make it hard for individuals and communities to be healthy. In this way, they are blind spots in communities—places that are neglected and not prioritized for investment, or that seem to linger almost indefinitely in a disappointing status quo, impervious to change.

High-speed traffic along streets with no sidewalks or with sidewalks adjacent to the roadway creates dangerous conditions for pedestrians. (Denver, Colorado)

Vista Avenue, Boise, Idaho

Federal Boulevard, Denver, Colorado

Corridors Participating in ULI's Healthy Corridors Project

Charlotte Avenue, Nashville, Tennessee

Van Nuys Boulevard, Pacoima, Los Angeles, California

Rice Street, spanning St. Paul, Roseville, and Maplewood, Minnesota

Grays Ferry Avenue, Philadelphia, Pennsylvania

ULI Healthy Corridors Project

Since 2014, ULI has been working with communities around the country through its district council (local chapter) network to help communities transform corridors into healthier places for the people who live, work, and travel along them.[1]

Along the demonstration corridors where ULI has been working, car-oriented street design makes it difficult or unsafe for people to walk or cross the street; a lack of well-maintained sidewalks and reliable public transit options gives people no choice except to drive; crosswalks are scarce; and people have no convenient access to healthy foods.

Despite these challenges, there is a real hunger for change, and many stakeholders throughout the country have come together to push for meaningful shifts in how these corridors function and serve their communities.

The ULI Healthy Corridors Project has allowed ULI and its partners to explore how to use health considerations to prioritize plans and investments that improve corridor conditions.

This Report

Though communities all over the country host underperforming and unhealthy arterial streets, until this study there had been no comprehensive look at the prevalence and location of unhealthy corridors, the conditions they share and the impact that they have on people's lives, or the policy and practice decisions that give rise to and perpetuate their existence.

To better understand the problem of unhealthy corridors, ULI and SGA launched a collaborative research project to answer the following questions:

- **What elements define unhealthy corridors, and what characteristics do they share?**
- **Are unhealthy corridors more concentrated in certain places and less concentrated in others?**
- **Who is most affected by unhealthy corridor conditions in terms of transportation, economics, health and safety, and equity?**
- **What policy decisions and practices contribute to unhealthy corridors?**

In answering these questions, ULI and SGA hope to add urgency to efforts to improve arterial corridors around the country. By understanding just how common the problem of unhealthy corridors is, where and how unhealthy corridors are most concentrated, and why these conditions persist, we can change the way we think about the challenges our streets face and illuminate a better way forward for healthier arterial corridors.

College Avenue, Fayetteville, Arkansas

South Broadway, Englewood, Colorado

Above: Many municipal parking ordinances require a minimum number of parking spaces per square foot of retail space. This can result in storefronts being separated from the street by a sea of parking. (Rice-Larpenteur Gateway in the St. Paul/Maplewood/Roseville, Minnesota, area)

Right: In the absence of proper infrastructure, pedestrians will create their own paths along streets—sometimes called "desire lines." (St. Paul, Minnesota)

Reema Singh

Key Findings

To understand how common unhealthy corridors are nationwide as well as to learn more about the characteristics they share and the policies and practices that contribute to their creation, ULI and SGA analyzed commercial corridors around the country. ULI and SGA identified 12 characteristics of commercial corridors and then conducted an audit of 6,925 urban and suburban commercial arterials from 100 of the most populous U.S. metropolitan areas.

The research, which provides a statistically accurate portrait of corridors nationwide, resulted in the following key findings:

- **Primary arterials are dangerous.** These high-capacity, high-speed roads represent 157,033 miles of the nation's 4.2 million miles of roadways—just 4 percent of the total—but have accounted for almost 30 percent of traffic fatalities in recent years.[2]

- **People walking make up a disproportionate share of traffic deaths on arterial commercial corridors.** Nationwide, 15 percent of people killed in traffic crashes were walking, but on the commercial corridors analyzed in this report, people on foot account for 32 percent of traffic deaths.

- **Unhealthy corridors are ubiquitous.** Sixty-seven percent of commercial corridors are at least moderately unhealthy, and 4 percent are severely unhealthy. Only 3 percent can be considered healthy.

- **Unhealthy corridors constitute a loss to communities** in terms of human life and safety, economic productivity, and transportation efficiency.

- **Overlapping land use and transportation policies and practices lead to the proliferation and persistence of unhealthy corridors.** These policies and practices can and should be addressed so that corridors are better able to serve their communities.

An Urgent Opportunity

With this research project, ULI, SGA, and the Robert Wood Johnson Foundation hope to add urgency to efforts to improve corridors around the country. When people understand just how common this problem is, where and how it is most concentrated, and why these conditions persist, they can change the way they think about the challenges their streets face and illuminate a better way forward for healthier corridors.

This research shows that unhealthy corridors can have major consequences for the health and well-being of the people who live, work, and travel along them, and for the economic and equity outcomes in communities. Unhealthy conditions are not inevitable for corridors; they are the result of accumulated policy and practice choices made by land use and transportation decision-makers now and in the past. With the right mix of interventions and political will, we can resolve the problems that persist along unhealthy corridors and transform them into healthier places for people.

—— Corridor Conditions Categories ——

Transportation	Street design Transit options Car use
Economics	Businesses Job density Land use
Health and safety	Healthy foods Air quality Traffic safety
Equity	Local opportunities Affordability Income segregation

FLAGSHIP MOTORS

DLR# 4779

1755 VISTA

1703 VISTA

AUTO METRIC

Foreign Car Service

"QUALITY USED CARS"
MECHANICS YOU CAN TRUST!

PARTS PLUS

CarCareCenter
Your Nationwide Neighborhood Garage

Part 1
Understanding Corridor Conditions

Measuring Unhealthy
Corridors

Key Findings

Facing page: Unhealthy corridors
are more likely to have land uses
and street design that emphasize
the automobile. (Boise, Idaho)

Measuring Unhealthy Corridors

To understand how common unhealthy corridors are nationwide as well as to learn more about the characteristics they share and the policies and practices that contribute to their creation, the report team developed a method to analyze commercial corridors around the country.

Defining Corridor Conditions

The report team identified 12 characteristics of commercial corridors nationwide to measure unhealthy conditions (see figure 1). These characteristics fall into four categories:

1) Transportation   3) Health and safety

2) Economics   4) Equity

This list is not exhaustive, but it represents the data currently available to measure unhealthy corridors nationwide.

Figure 1. Four Categories of Corridor Conditions

Transportation

Indicator	Unhealthy corridor conditions	Healthy corridor conditions
Street design Density and design of the street network	Street design prioritizes moving cars as quickly as possible, with long blocks and multiple, wide lanes.	Street design ensures that all people can safely share the street with narrow travel lanes and lower speed limits.
Transit options Proximity of jobs to bus stops, rail stations, and other fixed public transit	Access to public transportation is limited or nonexistent. If any public transit exists, it is more than a 10-minute walk from most people's place of work.	Public transit is directly accessible: many people's places of work are within about a 10-minute walk of a bus stop, rail station, or other type of public transit.
Car use Nearby residents who commute to work by driving alone	A high percentage of people who live along or near the corridor tend to drive to work alone. Other travel alternatives may be inconvenient, unsafe, or inaccessible.	People who live along or near the corridor get to work using a variety of travel modes, including walking, biking, riding public transit, and carpooling. As a result, a smaller percentage of people commute to work by driving alone.

Economics

Indicator	Unhealthy corridor conditions	Healthy corridor conditions
Businesses Vacancy rates for nearby commercial properties	The corridor has many empty storefronts.	Almost all storefronts along the corridor are occupied by businesses.
Job density Commercial jobs per acre	Few job opportunities exist along the corridor, and those that do are spread over a wide area.	Many job opportunities exist along the corridor within walking distance of one another.
Land use Balance of residential and commercial uses	Land along or near the corridor is separated by use. Most land is commercial with little or no residential use nearby. As a result, people tend to live farther from where they work and shop.	Land along or near the corridor includes a mix of residential and commercial uses. As a result, people tend to live closer to the places where they work and shop, making it easier to walk or bike to these places.

Data Limitations

Other factors—for which data are not available on a national scale—also contribute to unhealthy corridor conditions. For instance, though the National Highway Traffic Safety Administration maintains comprehensive national data on traffic deaths, data on traffic injuries nationwide are not available.

Also, unhealthy corridors tend to lack street trees, parks, and other green infrastructure to mitigate heat and stormwater flows. They also may lack sidewalks and crosswalks, or such pedestrian infrastructure may be poorly maintained, inaccessible to people with disabilities, or obstructed by above-ground utility poles and signs. They may be affected by noise and pollution, and they may have challenges with water and wastewater infrastructure.

But because no data are available on these conditions, they do not factor into the corridor grades in this report. Nonetheless, ULI and SGA encourage communities to consider these aspects when identifying and improving their corridors.

Health and Safety

	Indicator	Unhealthy corridor conditions	Healthy corridor conditions
3	**Healthy foods** Proximity of grocery stores to nearby residents	People living along or near the corridor are not within a 10-minute walk of a grocery store.	People living along or near the corridor are within a 10-minute walk of a large grocery store.
	Air quality Carbon dioxide emissions from transportation, per acre	Greenhouse gas emissions from transportation are relatively high along the corridor. As a result, people who live or work along the corridor may be exposed to poor air quality and experience higher risks of asthma and other respiratory diseases.	Greenhouse gas emissions from transportation are relatively low along the corridor, which can lead to better air quality and a lower risk of asthma and other respiratory diseases.
	Traffic safety Deaths from traffic crashes	Fatal crashes cluster along or near the corridor.	The corridor is safe for all users and has no history of fatal crashes.

Equity

	Indicator	Unhealthy corridor conditions	Healthy corridor conditions
4	**Local opportunities** People who live and work within the same census tract	Few or no people who live along or near the corridor work along the corridor.	People who live along or near the corridor benefit from local job opportunities.
	Affordability Percentage of household income spent on housing and transportation	People who live along or near the corridor spend a disproportionate share of their income on housing and transportation.	People who live along or near the corridor spend a relatively small share of their income on housing and transportation.
	Income segregation Income distribution of nearby residents	Housing along or near the corridor is segregated by income level.	Housing along or near the corridor serves a variety of income levels.

Corridor Audit

Building on ULI's previous work on healthy corridors and the corridor conditions defined here, ULI and SGA conducted an audit of 6,925 urban and suburban commercial arterials from 100 of the most populous U.S. metropolitan areas. (Five were excluded from this study because they had fewer than five commercial corridors in the sample.)

The corridors included in this audit are all classified by the Federal Highway Administration as "other principal arterials"—major arterial roads excluding interstates, freeways, and expressways.

Though these types of high-capacity, high-speed roads account for only 4 percent of the total U.S. roadway miles, almost 30 percent of traffic fatalities occurred on them.

FIGURE 2. Concentration of Traffic Deaths on Arterial Roads Nationwide

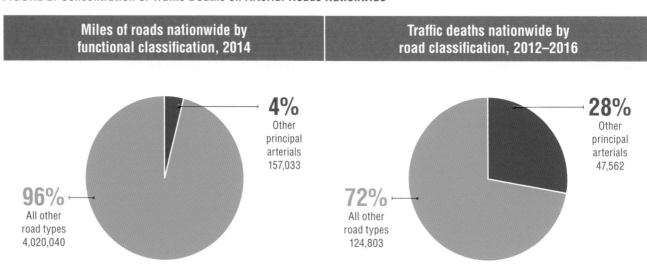

Miles of roads nationwide by functional classification, 2014	Traffic deaths nationwide by road classification, 2012–2016

4%
Other principal arterials
157,033

96%
All other road types
4,020,040

28%
Other principal arterials
47,562

72%
All other road types
124,803

Sources: Federal Highway Administration, "Highway Statistics 2014," 2014; National Highway Traffic Safety Administration, "Fatality Analysis Reporting System (FARS) Encyclopedia," 2018.

Nearly 30 percent of traffic fatalities occurred on pedestrian-unfriendly urban and suburban arterials, even though these streets represent only 4 percent of total U.S. roadways. (Fayetteville, Arkansas)

FIGURE 3. Categorizing Corridor Conditions

Corridor condition	Description	Score out of 120
Severely unhealthy	Corridors scoring poorly in all four categories; they are automobile oriented and inequitable, underperform economically, and have low ratings for health and safety.	40 or lower
Moderately unhealthy	Corridors scoring poorly in two or three categories and underperforming overall in terms of transportation, economics, health and safety, and/or equity.	41 to 60
Moderately healthy	Corridors performing well in some categories but with unrealized potential in terms of transportation, economics, health and safety, and/or equity.	61 to 79
Healthy	Corridors receiving the highest grades; they are pedestrian oriented, equitable, economically vibrant, and supportive of health and safety.	80 or higher

ULI and SGA drew on national data sources to grade these corridors according to the 12 characteristics in the four categories of corridor conditions—transportation, economics, health and safety, and equity. Each of these categories accounted for 30 points, with each of the 12 indicators receiving a score from zero to 10 points for a total possible score of 120.

Those rated *severely unhealthy* corridors scored 40 points or less, *moderately unhealthy corridors* scored 41 to 60 points, *moderately healthy corridors* scored 61 to 79 points, and those scoring 80 points or more were rated *healthy corridors*.

For a more detailed explanation of the data sources and methodologies for sampling and grading corridors, consult the online appendixes at **www.uli.org/healthycorridors**.

Severely unhealthy corridors are automobile oriented, economically underperforming, and generally unsafe for pedestrians and bicyclists. (Philadelphia, Pennsylvania)

Key Findings

The ULI and SGA audit of commercial corridor segments provided the following insights into commercial corridor characteristics, their prevalence and location, their consequences, and who is most affected by them.

What Are the Characteristics of Commercial Corridors?

Overall, commercial corridors perform poorly in the equity and transportation categories. Severely unhealthy corridors perform especially poorly in transportation and in health and safety.

On average, commercial corridors in cities and suburbs nationwide fare poorly when it comes to transportation and equity. Across all corridors considered in the audit, average scores for transportation and equity were only 11.7 and 12.6 out of 30, respectively, compared with 17.0 for economics and 15.5 for health and safety. Severely unhealthy corridors in particular performed worst in transportation than in any other category.

Transit access, in particular, is lacking across all commercial corridors in the audit: 83 percent of corridors offer no access to transit within a half mile, and only 3 percent offer complete or near-complete access. (*Complete or near-complete access* is defined as meaning at least 90 percent of jobs along these corridors are located within half a mile of a transit stop.)

Access to healthy foods is also extremely limited on commercial corridors overall. On about half the commercial corridors in this audit, over 70 percent of people do not live within a half mile of a grocery store.

On average, 10 percent of businesses on these commercial corridors experienced vacancy at some point over a three-month period in 2014, and the vacancy rate ranges anywhere from zero to 64 percent. On almost 9 percent of corridors, at least one in five businesses is vacant.

Figure 4. Average Score for Commercial Corridors by Category

Category	All commercial corridors Sample size = 6,925	Severely unhealthy corridors Sample size = 289
Transportation	11.7 out of 30	6.5 out of 30
Economics	17.0 out of 30	14.1 out of 30
Health and safety	15.5 out of 30	8.9 out of 30
Equity	12.6 out of 30	8.1 out of 30
Overall	**56.7 out of 120**	**37.7 out of 120**

Source: ULI and SGA corridor audit data.

83% of audited corridors offer no access to transit within a half mile.

10% of businesses on audited commercial corridors are vacant, on average.

How Prevalent Are Unhealthy Corridors, and Where Are They Located?

More than two-thirds of commercial arterials are at least moderately unhealthy. Very few corridors— only 3 percent—qualify as healthy.

The scoring process revealed that two-thirds of commercial arterials in cities and suburbs around the country are at least moderately unhealthy. Four percent of corridors are severely unhealthy, and 63 percent are moderately unhealthy. In comparison, only 3 percent of corridors are healthy, and 30 percent are moderately healthy.

Facing page: Access to healthy food, including grocery stores, is very limited on commercial corridors. (Fayetteville, Arkansas)

Figure 5. Commercial Corridor Conditions Nationwide

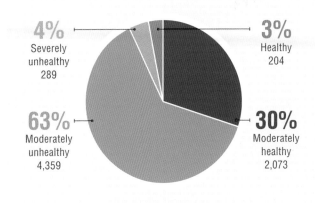

4% Severely unhealthy 289

3% Healthy 204

63% Moderately unhealthy 4,359

30% Moderately healthy 2,073

Sample size = 6,925 corridors

Source: ULI and SGA corridor audit data.

Unhealthy corridors are more common in the southern United States than in the north.

The northern regions of the United States have healthier commercial corridors overall than do the southern regions. Specifically, the Northwest, West, and Northeast have higher shares of healthy corridors and smaller shares of moderately or severely unhealthy corridors than do other regions.

The Southwest has the highest proportion of corridors rated severely unhealthy, and almost 75 percent of corridors in the Southeast are at least moderately unhealthy.

The most sprawling metropolitan areas are concentrated in the southern United States,[3] and these places tend to have higher shares of moderately or severely unhealthy corridors. Many factors may contribute to these trends, but in general these regions were built on the scale of the car, so they tend to have networks of dangerously wide, high-speed roadways and sprawling patterns of land use.

Figure 6. Distribution of Unhealthy Corridors by Region

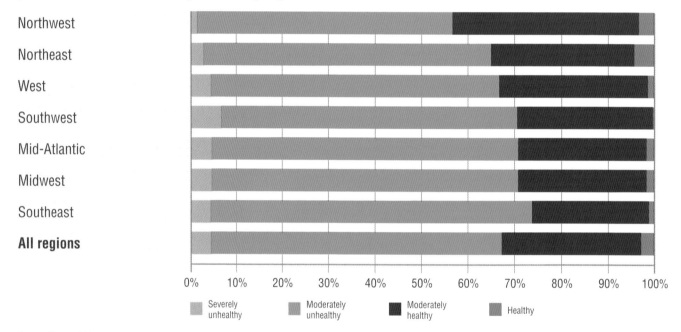

Source: ULI and SGA corridor audit data.

Urban corridors tend to be healthier than suburban corridors.

Commercial corridors within the city limits of major metropolitan regions tend to be healthier than their suburban counterparts. Half the corridors in cities are moderately or severely unhealthy, compared with about three-quarters of those in suburbs. Furthermore, 12 percent of corridors in cities are healthy, compared with only 1 percent of corridors in suburbs.

In their overall scores on corridor health, urban commercial corridors score significantly higher overall and in the transportation, economics, and equity categories. Specifically, cities score on average about five points higher on the 120-point scale (total points) than do suburban corridors. In the transportation category, urban commercial corridors score on average more than three points higher on the 30-point scale (category points) than do suburban corridors.

Figure 7. Commercial Corridor Conditions in Cities versus Suburbs

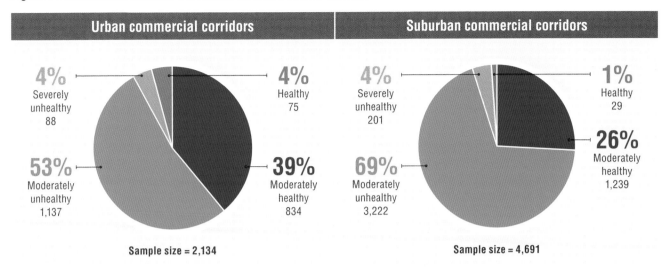

Urban commercial corridors

- **4%** Severely unhealthy 88
- **4%** Healthy 75
- **53%** Moderately unhealthy 1,137
- **39%** Moderately healthy 834

Sample size = 2,134

Suburban commercial corridors

- **4%** Severely unhealthy 201
- **1%** Healthy 29
- **26%** Moderately healthy 1,239
- **69%** Moderately unhealthy 3,222

Sample size = 4,691

Source: ULI and SGA corridor audit data.

What Are the Consequences of Unhealthy Corridors?

Commercial arterials are dangerous, especially for people walking or biking.

Between 2012 and 2016, 47,562 people died on primary arterials (excluding interstates, freeways, and expressways) nationwide, accounting for 28 percent of traffic fatalities. On the 6,925 commercial corridor segments analyzed in this report,

8,572 people died during the same period. Of those deaths, 2,727 involved people walking and 329 were people biking.[4]

People walking and biking in particular make up a disproportionate share of deaths on commercial arterials. Nationwide, 15 percent of people killed in traffic crashes between 2012 and 2016 were walking, but on commercial corridors, people walking made up 32 percent of deaths. Similarly, people biking accounted for 2 percent of fatalities nationwide but 4 percent of deaths on the commercial corridors analyzed in this report.[5]

Figure 8. Traffic Deaths by Mode of Transportation, 2012–2016

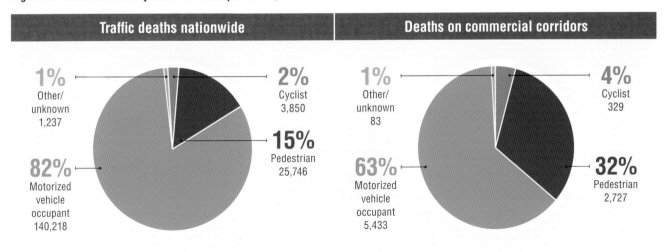

Traffic deaths nationwide

- **1%** Other/unknown 1,237
- **2%** Cyclist 3,850
- **15%** Pedestrian 25,746
- **82%** Motorized vehicle occupant 140,218

Deaths on commercial corridors

- **1%** Other/unknown 83
- **4%** Cyclist 329
- **32%** Pedestrian 2,727
- **63%** Motorized vehicle occupant 5,433

Sources: ULI and SGA corridor audit data; National Highway Traffic Safety Administration, "Fatality Analysis Reporting System (FARS) Encyclopedia," 2017.

Who Is Most Affected by Unhealthy Corridors?

People of Latino ethnicity and older adults are dying in disproportionate numbers in traffic crashes along severely unhealthy corridors.

Nationwide, a disproportionate number of people of Latino ethnicity and older adults die in traffic crashes in general, and these disparities are even more pronounced on commercial corridors.

About 13 percent of people killed in traffic crashes across the country from 2012 to 2016 are Latino, but on severely unhealthy corridors, people in this group make up almost 17 percent of deaths.

The *fatality rate* for people of Latino ethnicity is also higher on severely unhealthy corridors than across the nation as a whole. From 2012 to 2016, Latino people on all roads died at a rate of 13.8 per 10,000 Latino workers, but on severely unhealthy corridors this rate was as high as 18.8 per 10,000 jobs held by Latino individuals. (Because commercial corridors tend to have few residences, this statistic uses workers as a proxy for population density.)

Figure 9: Latino Share of Traffic Deaths Nationwide and on Severely Unhealthy Corridors, 2012–2016

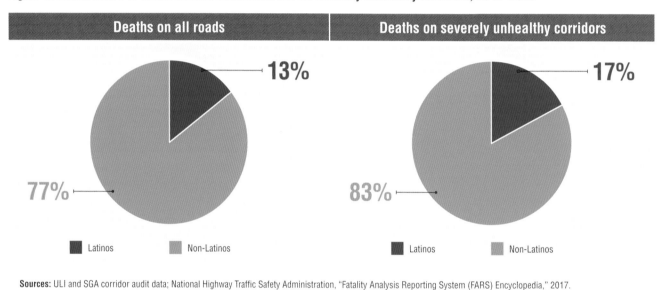

Sources: ULI and SGA corridor audit data; National Highway Traffic Safety Administration, "Fatality Analysis Reporting System (FARS) Encyclopedia," 2017.

Figure 10: Latino Fatality Rate per 10,000 Jobs on All Roads, Commercial Corridors, and Severely Unhealthy Corridors, 2012–2016

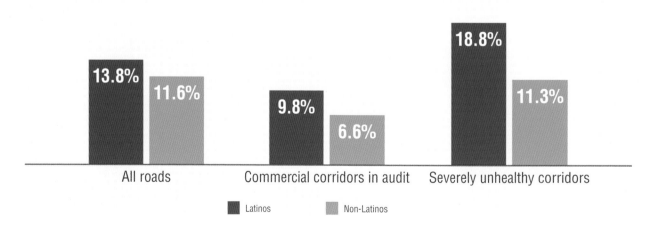

Sources: ULI and SGA corridor audit data; National Highway Traffic Safety Administration, "Fatality Analysis Reporting System (FARS) Encyclopedia," 2017.

Similarly, older adults are especially susceptible to dying in traffic crashes on severely unhealthy corridors. On severely unhealthy corridors, 34 percent of people killed are age 55 and over; this age group accounts for 31 percent of deaths in all traffic crashes nationwide.

The *fatality rate* for older adults is also higher on severely unhealthy corridors than across the nation as a whole. From 2012 to 2016, older people on all roads died at a rate of 18.6 per 10,000 older workers, but on severely unhealthy corridors this rate was as high as 22.5 per 10,000 jobs

held by older adults. Looked at another way, even though only 19 percent of people who work along commercial corridors are age 55 or older, this group accounts for more than one-third of all traffic deaths in these places.

Conversely, people age 29 or younger account for a slightly smaller share of deaths on commercial corridors overall and on severely unhealthy corridors, compared with all traffic crashes. For people age 30 to 54, the fatality rate is about the same for deaths per worker on severely unhealthy commercial corridors and in all traffic crashes.

Figure 11: Older-Adult Share of Traffic Deaths Nationwide and on Severely Unhealthy Corridors, 2012–2016

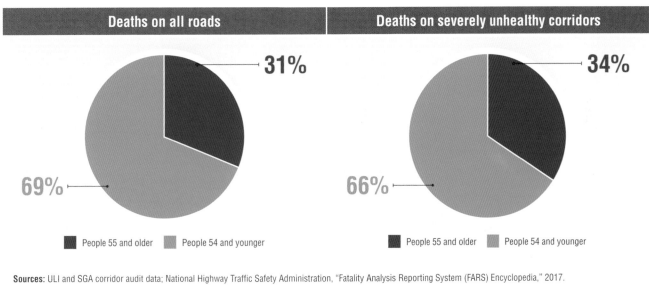

Sources: ULI and SGA corridor audit data; National Highway Traffic Safety Administration, "Fatality Analysis Reporting System (FARS) Encyclopedia," 2017.

Figure 12: Fatality Rate per 10,000 Jobs by Age Group on All Roads, Commercial Corridors, and Severely Unhealthy Corridors, 2012–2016

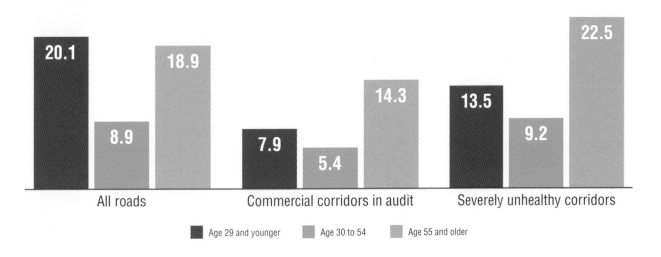

Sources: ULI and SGA corridor audit data; National Highway Traffic Safety Administration, "Fatality Analysis Reporting System (FARS) Encyclopedia," 2017.

Low-income people working along unhealthy corridors earn less than they would working elsewhere.

Although people who work along severely unhealthy corridors have a similar level of education as the workforce nationwide, they tend to earn less than they would working elsewhere.

Nationwide, about 20 percent of workers earn $1,250 or less per month, but along severely unhealthy corridors, 30 percent of workers make $1,250 or less. Conversely, along healthy corridors, workers tend to be better educated and earn higher salaries. More than half the people who work along healthy corridors earn at least $3,333 per month, while only about one-third of workers along severely unhealthy corridors receive wages this high.

Figure 13. Job Distribution by Level of Education, Nationwide and by Corridor Condition

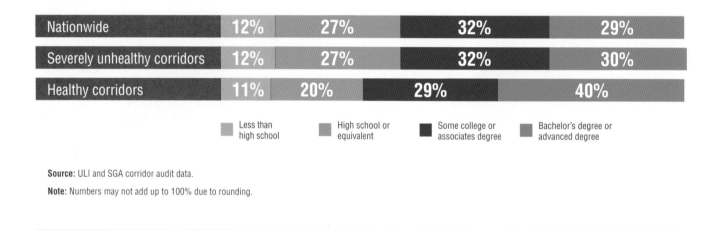

	Less than high school	High school or equivalent	Some college or associates degree	Bachelor's degree or advanced degree
Nationwide	12%	27%	32%	29%
Severely unhealthy corridors	12%	27%	32%	30%
Healthy corridors	11%	20%	29%	40%

Source: ULI and SGA corridor audit data.

Note: Numbers may not add up to 100% due to rounding.

Figure 14. Monthly Income, Nationwide and by Corridor Condition

	Earn $1,250 or less	Earn $1,251 to $3,333	Earn $3,333 or more
Nationwide	20%	36%	44%
Severely unhealthy corridors	30%	35%	35%
Healthy corridors	20%	26%	54%

Source: ULI and SGA corridor audit data.

Facing page: Bicyclists and pedestrians are at particular risk of being killed along unhealthy corridors. "Ghost bikes" mark sites of deadly crashes. Here, a ghost bike along Van Nuys Boulevard in Los Angeles memorializes the death of a cyclist.

Rachel MacCleery

Part 2
Causes and Solutions

Policies and Practices

From Unhealthy to
Healthy Corridors

Policies and Practices

The results of the corridor audit reinforce what people already know: the problem of unhealthy corridors is widespread in the United States. Why is this the case? What are communities doing that consistently creates and perpetuates these conditions?

To answer these questions, the report team engaged transportation, land use, and health experts to identify the policies and practices that contribute to the problem.

Longstanding policies and practices for commercial corridors make it challenging for people using modes of transportation other than motor vehicles to navigate the street. (**Facing page:** Philadelphia, Pennsylvania; **below:** Fayetteville, Arkansas)

Among the key policy decisions and institutional practices that create, perpetuate, and exacerbate unhealthy corridors are the following:

- Land use regulations that separate residential from commercial places and establish excessive parking requirements.

- Street design guidelines and performance measures that emphasize moving cars as quickly as possible rather than investments in people-oriented mobility infrastructure.

- Assessment-based tax policies that discourage private investment and development.

- Lack of local autonomy over and input on the design and operation of arterial roadways.

This chapter examines these decisions and practices, and provides snapshots of typical unhealthy corridors affected by them. These examples do not necessarily represent the most extreme or egregious cases of unhealthy corridors, but rather are fairly typical of the policies, practices, and resulting corridor conditions observed across the United States—and perhaps even in your own community.

Sprawling, Separated Land Use Patterns and Related Policies

Cities and towns adopt zoning codes that determine where private developers and public entities can locate different kinds of buildings. **Most communities, especially suburbs, have single-use or Euclidean zoning policies, which separate residences from commercial and industrial buildings.** Under this type of land use regulation, homes tend to be far from jobs, schools, shops, churches, and places of recreation. Therefore, it may be difficult, inconvenient, or even unsafe to walk, bike, or ride public transit, leaving people with no alternative except to drive.

Minimum parking requirements often exacerbate these sprawling, separated land use conditions by requiring that too much space be devoted to parking. Many towns and cities have parking ordinances that establish a minimum number of parking spaces for each particular type of development. For example, a restaurant or store may be required to provide at least a certain number of parking spaces per square foot of dining or retail space, or an apartment or office building may have to provide a certain number of spaces per unit.

These parking minimums, usually the product of outdated formulas or designed to satisfy demand on the busiest day of the year, can result in commercial corridors where storefronts are set far back from the roadway behind seas of underused parking. In addition, paving over so much ground to accommodate parked cars can lead to negative environmental impacts that include heat islands, poor air quality, and flooding from a lack of permeable surface to help process stormwater.

Alternative Approaches

As an alternative to single-use zoning, **some communities have established mixed-use zoning districts or require ground-floor commercial space in apartment buildings.** Mixed-use zoning policies mean the local government allows residential and commercial places to exist next to each other or even directly on top of one another. As a result, the places where people live tend to be closer to the places where they work, shop, and learn, often making it easier to walk, bike, or ride transit to these places.

Other communities—including Beaufort, South Carolina; Nashville, Tennessee; Arlington, Virginia; and many others—have gone a step further by adopting **form-based codes**, which allow them to regulate the form rather than use of buildings.[6] For example, form-based codes can require storefronts to be located closer to the roadway with parking at the rear rather than in front of the building, which creates denser, more walkable places.

Other strategies to reduce unnecessarily large parking lots include revising parking ordinances to establish **parking maximums** rather than minimums or carrying out infill development by replacing underused parking lots with new residential, commercial, or mixed-use buildings located closer to the street.

Form-based codes, applied here along Columbia Pike in Arlington, Virginia, can require storefronts to be located adjacent to the sidewalk with parking in the rear.

Google Street View

Corridor Snapshot

Denton Highway
Haltom City, Texas

Denton Highway is the typical outcome of local separated land use policies and excessive parking minimums. The city zoned the corridor exclusively for commercial and industrial uses.[7] Though a residential neighborhood is located immediately east of Denton Highway, no complete sidewalk connections exist between this corridor and the neighborhood, and along the vast majority of Denton Highway there are no sidewalks at all.

Haltom City's parking ordinance, in keeping with common practice for many towns and cities, requires stores to have a minimum of one parking space for every 200 square feet of retail space and at least one space for every three seats of restaurant seating.[8] As a result, businesses along Denton Highway are set far back from the street behind large, mostly underused parking lots.

Between Straightaway Drive and Glenview Drive, surface parking lots occupy almost three-fourths of the commercial space along Denton Highway, with significant consequences for the air quality: the carbon dioxide emissions per acre along Denton Highway are more than double the average emissions for the commercial corridors audited for this report.

DENTON HIGHWAY SCORECARD

Corridor characteristic	Corridor score per characteristic	Average for all commercial corridors
Corridor score	**37 / 120**	**56.7 / 120**
Transportation	4 / 30	11.7 / 30
Economics	4 / 30	17.0 / 30
Health and safety	14 / 30	15.5 / 30
Equity	15 / 30	12.6 / 30

OTHER DENTON HIGHWAY DATA

Jobs accessible via transit	0%
Percentage driving alone to work	96%
Lack of access to healthy foods	53%
Traffic deaths over five years	0
Vacancy rate	26%
Cost of housing and transportation as percentage of household income	44%
CO_2 emissions per acre (metric tons)	30.4

◼ Severely unhealthy ◼ Moderately unhealthy ◻ Moderately healthy ◼ Healthy

Right: Surface parking (highlighted in blue) along Denton Highway occupies almost three-fourths of the commercial space between Straightaway Drive and Glenview Drive.

Far right: Starlight Drive extends from Denton Highway into a nearby residential neighborhood. However, there are no complete sidewalk connections between the neighborhood and the commercial corridor. A half-block sidewalk to nowhere stretches from the driveway of a car wash to the edge of a vacant lot but reaches neither the intersection with Denton Highway nor the residential neighborhood.

Google Street View with ULI and SGA analysis

Google Street View

Car-Oriented Street Design and Operations

In every step of the transportation planning process, cars tend to take precedence over people walking, biking, or riding public transit. When it comes to allocating funds to transportation projects, many states and local and regional jurisdictions consistently spend most of their budgets on roadway widening and maintenance projects, whereas investment in walking, biking, and public transit remains minimal to nonexistent.

In some cases, this funding allocation results from formal criteria for project selection that focus on roadway level of service, a standard transportation performance measure that defines the success of a roadway entirely by the absence of traffic congestion. However, even in cases where formal criteria to guide project selection do not exist, many decision-makers continue to fund projects that benefit cars through their informal decision-making practices, whereas investment in walking, biking, and public transit is perceived as superfluous or unnecessary.

In addition to car-oriented project selection, **commonly accepted street design guidelines often fail to address how people walking, biking, and riding transit, including those with mobility challenges, can safely share the road with cars.**

For example, two street design guides that engineers continue to rely on are *A Policy on Geometric Design of Highways and Streets,* widely known as the Green Book, from the American Association of State Highway and Transportation Officials (AASHTO), and the *Manual on Uniform Traffic Control Devices* (MUTCD) from the Federal Highway Administration.

Until recent editions, these guides failed to sufficiently incorporate walking and biking beyond providing suggestions on minimum sidewalk widths. They continue to call for wide lanes and a wide turning radius at intersections to accommodate large trucks but do not provide much information about how to incorporate safe crosswalks at intersections or at midblock.

"Most of the facilities needed for bicycle travel can consist of the street and highway system generally as it presently exists."

— AASHTO Green Book, Fourth Edition, 2001

Although recent efforts to update these resources have included development of separate, specialized guidance for bikeways, the car-oriented best practices ingrained in these design guides remain common practice among many engineers across the country. Transportation department priorities reflect these biases.

Alternative Approaches

More than 1,300 communities around the country have adopted **Complete Streets** policies that commit to creating comprehensive networks to support walking, biking, and use of public transit.[9] The strongest Complete Streets policies call for binding actions to change internal policies and practices that currently prioritize cars. One such action is **creating or adopting multimodal design guidance that takes into account the context of the street,** including traffic speed and surrounding land use. A resource providing such guidance is the *Urban Street Design Guide* from the National Association of City Transportation Officials (NACTO).

The best Complete Streets policies establish project-selection criteria and performance measures that move beyond level of service to consider the safe movement of all people who use the street regardless of mode of transportation. Such criteria and measures are laid out in the report *Evaluating Complete Streets Projects: A Guide for Practitioners,* produced by AARP, SGA, and the National Complete Streets Coalition.

Included in a $146 million investment in Aurora Avenue in Shoreline, Washington, dedicated bus lanes and other improvements have increased ridership and safety.

Google Street View

Corridor Snapshot

Clinton Highway
Knoxville, Tennessee

Unlike many of the severely unhealthy corridors in the ULI/SGA audit, Clinton Highway has some land use conditions that could support walkability. Though many of the businesses along this corridor are located behind the seas of parking typical for unhealthy corridors, some storefronts are very close to the road.

However, this five- to six-lane road with a speed limit of 50 miles per hour is designed exclusively to move cars as quickly as possible. Despite the wide buffers of green space that run alongside much of the road, including a limited number of street trees, there are no sidewalks, crosswalks, public transit stops, or bikeways.

Under current conditions, it is dangerous to walk, bike, or even drive on Clinton Highway. People have been struck and killed while walking along the roadway, including as recently as December 2017, when a driver struck and killed a pedestrian and received no formal charge or citation.[10]

Transforming this high-speed throughway into a healthier commercial corridor would require Knoxville to collaborate with the Tennessee Department of Transportation to overhaul the design of the street to prioritize all people who use it. For example, this could mean reducing the width and number of lanes; introducing separated, shared walking and biking paths; bringing more businesses closer to the road; and planting additional street trees and other landscaping features.

CLINTON HIGHWAY SCORECARD

Corridor characteristic	Corridor score per characteristic	Average for all commercial corridors
Corridor score	**40 / 120**	**56.7 / 120**
Transportation	7 / 30	11.7 / 30
Economics	19 / 30	17.0 / 30
Health and safety	8 / 30	15.5 / 30
Equity	6 / 30	12.6 / 30

OTHER CLINTON HIGHWAY DATA

Jobs accessible via transit	0%
Percentage driving alone to work	90%
Lack of access to healthy foods	84%
Traffic deaths over five years	2
Vacancy rate	6%
Cost of housing and transportation as percentage of household income	61%
CO_2 emissions per acre (metric tons)	10.2

Severely unhealthy   Moderately unhealthy   Moderately healthy   Healthy

Clinton Highway is designed exclusively to move as many cars as quickly as possible. The corridor has the potential to become a more walkable, bikeable, transit-accessible place, but this would require significant city cooperation with the state department of transportation to undertake a wholesale redesign.

Google Street View

Disincentives to Private Development

If a corridor is severely unhealthy, with high vacancy rates and deteriorated buildings, it can be difficult for a community to attract new private investment. Corridors can fall into a state of decline for many reasons, and these reasons vary substantially from place to place.

However, **federal tax policies can exacerbate these conditions by making it even more challenging for unhealthy corridors to recover.** For example, the Internal Revenue Service (IRS) allows landowners to claim tax deductions on vacant land but not to write off any improvements made to these vacant properties. This policy creates financial incentives for land to remain vacant, particularly along corridors that are already unhealthy where improvements might be considered a risky investment.

In addition, the IRS can attach tax liens to vacant buildings whose owners are unable to continue paying property taxes, making it difficult or impossible to sell those buildings to other business owners or developers who might reoccupy and improve those spaces.

Also, commonly used assessment-based tax policies calculate property taxes based on the value of the property, including any buildings or amenities on it. This means **a landowner who makes improvements to a property will see the taxes on that property increase accordingly.**

Along unhealthy corridors where such investments may present short-term risk, this can discourage property owners from maintaining or improving commercial spaces. Alternatively, a property owner that does make improvements may make up for the added taxes by increasing rents, which can displace existing businesses.

Alternative Approaches

To overcome disinvestment along unhealthy corridors, **some communities have adopted policies that penalize absentee property owners for sitting on vacant land.** For example, jurisdictions can impose annual registration fees for vacant properties and buildings.

Alternatively, jurisdictions like Pittsburgh have had success encouraging investment by moving away from assessment-based taxation or supplementing it with land-value tax policies that encourage property owners not to leave land vacant and allow them to make storefront improvements without being penalized.[11]

Other initiatives that can attract investment to underserved commercial corridors include providing **small-scale loans and grants to local business owners to help them purchase the spaces they rent and improve their storefronts,** as well as establishing programs that provide training and support to aspiring business owners.

Programs that provide loans or grants to help local businesses improve storefronts or purchase the spaces they rent can help increase investment along commercial corridors. (Fayetteville, Arkansas)

Google Street View

Corridor Snapshot

West Fifth Avenue

Gary, Indiana

West Fifth Avenue is bordered on both sides by parking lots and unmarked or vacant stores. The roadway is made up of four to five wide lanes and a plain concrete median, but has few or no curbs, little in the way of green infrastructure, and few sidewalks. Along the section of West Fifth Avenue included in the unhealthy corridors audit, vacancy rates are as high as 36 percent.

These conditions are not unique to this corridor in Gary. "Gary Counts," a citywide survey of properties conducted by the city in collaboration with the University of Chicago, found that almost 25 percent of commercial properties are vacant, and nearly another 50 percent are in a very poor state of repair.[12]

These conditions are the result of broader economic issues facing the city. Originally a steel town, Gary experienced deindustrialization that left the city in a state of serious decline. Massive job and population losses, including the departure of white and comparatively wealthy residents, led to many abandoned properties and vacant school buildings, many of which are difficult or impossible to sell due to federal liens placed on them by the IRS.[13] These issues are compounded by a rise in vandalism, leaving Gary with a reputation for blight and crime.

The city, with support from the state, has taken steps to encourage revitalization. The state established a regional development authority in an effort to attract investment to northwest Indiana, and the city has demolished a large number of vacant buildings through a state-funded program in the hope of making way for new development.[14]

However, Gary has a long way to go to reverse half a century of disinvestment and decline, and West Fifth Avenue, with its numerous wide lanes, massive swaths of underused parking, and lack of sidewalks, green infrastructure, and other amenities will make it challenging for the corridor to attract new investment.

WEST FIFTH AVENUE SCORECARD

Corridor characteristic	Corridor score per characteristic	Average for all commercial corridors
Corridor score	**40 / 120**	**56.7 / 120**
Transportation	5 / 30	11.7 / 30
Economics	2 / 30	17.0 / 30
Health and safety	20 / 30	15.5 / 30
Equity	13 / 30	12.6 / 30

OTHER WEST FIFTH AVENUE DATA	
Jobs accessible via transit	10%
Percentage driving alone to work	94%
Lack of access to healthy foods	100%
Traffic deaths over five years	0
Vacancy rate	36%
Cost of housing and transportation as percentage of household income	39%
CO_2 emissions per acre (metric tons)	0.5

Severely unhealthy   Moderately unhealthy   Moderately healthy   Healthy

Vacant land and poorly maintained properties are commonplace along West Fifth Avenue, reflecting larger trends in Gary.

Google Street View

Lack of Local Autonomy Over Roadways

Although arterial commercial corridors run through local jurisdictions, **state and county governments often own these roadways and base decisions regarding design and vehicle speed on priorities that may conflict with local goals.**

On one hand, these streets provide access to local stores, jobs, and amenities, but on the other, they often serve as major throughways for regional mobility. While lower speeds along commercial corridors create a safer environment more conducive to walking, biking, and window-shopping, high speeds provide convenience for through-traffic.

The state's or county's view of the corridor as a major route for commuters, as an emergency evacuation route in case of a disaster, or as an alternative route in the event of construction, car crashes, or other closures on major parallel routes can make it impossible to realize local visions for walkable, inviting main streets.

Alternative Approaches

Some towns and cities have succeeded in transforming state- or county-owned arterials into safer, local commercial corridors by agreeing to take over the cost of maintenance or ownership of the roadway. For example, Orlando negotiated with the Florida Department of Transportation for control of Edgewater Drive, which the city transformed into a safer, more walkable commercial corridor by reducing the number of travel lanes and adding bike lanes.[15]

In addition, some state departments of transportation are adopting more context-sensitive design guidance to give local governments more flexibility and autonomy. Context-sensitive design approaches seek to inform transportation planning with community values and perspectives and information about the surrounding land use context. The Tennessee Department of Transportation in 2018 created and adopted the *Multimodal Project Scoping Manual,* granting local and regional governments more flexibility to redesign and re-stripe roads in order to more safely accommodate all people who use the street, regardless of mode of transportation.[16]

Another way to address the widespread unhealthy corridor problem is sharing of power over roadways, giving local authorities more control over the speed, design, and operation of their streets. This approach might include introducing more lenient, context-sensitive design guidelines at the state and federal levels that give local jurisdictions more flexibility to calm traffic on the roads running through their communities.

In addition, **local organizations such as business improvement districts (BIDs) and other community associations can partner with cities** to introduce and maintain improvements to corridors that transform them into safer, greener, more economically vibrant, and healthier places for all people.

The transfer of ownership of roads from the state or county has allowed cities such as Orlando to improve streets to make them more walkable and bikeable.

Google Street View

Corridor Snapshot
Route 206
Hillsborough, New Jersey

In June 1999, Hillsborough adopted a master plan that reimagined Route 206 as a walkable, bikeable main street. The plan called for major changes that would transform the roadway into a healthier corridor, including traffic calming, infill development in the underused parking lots, a mix of housing and retail space along the corridor, a major transit center with a new commuter-rail station, and bicycle and pedestrian connections to adjacent neighborhoods.

However, almost two decades later, this severely unhealthy corridor remains as it was originally described in the 1999 master plan: a wide thoroughfare surrounded by parking lots. What went wrong?

Unfortunately, Hillsborough's vision for a healthier corridor was thwarted by several key decisions at the state level. To start, the commuter-rail station initially proposed for Hillsborough never came to fruition after the state chose to redirect the funds to road projects.[17]

Next, the state's and county's concerns about traffic congestion prevented Hillsborough from transforming Route 206 from a major thoroughfare into a local main street.[18]

For Hillsborough to calm traffic on the highway, the New Jersey Department of Transportation (NJDOT) required a bypass route to resolve congestion on the existing Route 206. The bypass has been under discussion since the mid-1970s, but construction did not begin until 2010 and will not be completed until fall 2020.[19] NJDOT has also planned two road-widening projects on existing Route 206 beginning in 2019, which will convert two miles of the would-be main street from two to four lanes with concrete medians, further solidifying its role as a major throughway.[20]

As a result, Hillsborough's vision for a walkable main street has not progressed. Instead, Route 206 remains a severely unhealthy corridor with seas of parking lots and few to no amenities for walking, biking, or using public transit.

ROUTE 206 SCORECARD

Corridor characteristic	Corridor score per characteristic	Average for all commercial corridors
Corridor score	**39 / 120**	**56.7 / 120**
Transportation	11 / 30	11.7 / 30
Economics	13 / 30	17.0 / 30
Health and safety	9 / 30	15.5 / 30
Equity	6 / 30	12.6 / 30

OTHER ROUTE 206 DATA

Jobs accessible via transit	<1%
Percentage driving alone to work	88%
Lack of access to healthy foods	82%
Traffic deaths over five years	3
Vacancy rate	14%
Cost of housing and transportation as percentage of household income	73%
CO_2 emissions per acre (metric tons)	6.8

Severely unhealthy   Moderately unhealthy   Moderately healthy   Healthy

The presence of sidewalks along Route 206 is inconsistent, and they often end abruptly. Where this occurs, trails can be found worn into the roadside where people continue to walk to reach their destinations.

Google Street View

Left: A focus on arts, culture, and programming transformed High Street in Columbus, Ohio, from a neglected area with vacant buildings into a popular destination.

Below: Strategies that improve conditions for pedestrians and bicyclists should be a component of all transportation plans. (Englewood, Colorado)

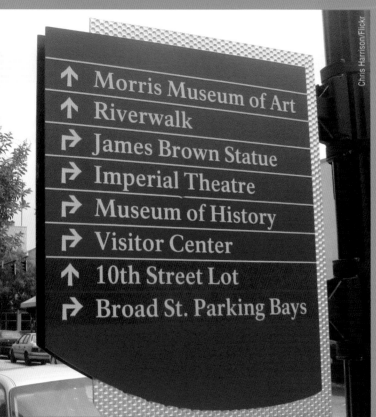

Above: Wayfinding tools such as pedestrian-focused signage should be used in conjunction with improved pedestrian and bike infrastructure. (Augusta, Georgia)

Right: Wide sidewalks buffered from vehicle lanes provide additional safety measures for pedestrians. (Shoreline, Washington)

Summary of Alternative Approaches

As this chapter makes clear, the unhealthy conditions common along many corridors today are the result of specific land use and transportation decisions made by communities and government agencies over the past few decades. These conditions are not inevitable, though they can seem that way. Opportunities exist every day to reverse course and make things better for the people and communities who are harmed by unhealthy corridors.

To begin improving their corridors, communities can take the following actions.

To address sprawling, separated land use patterns:

- Replace single-use zoning with mixed-use zoning districts or require ground-floor commercial space in apartment buildings.

- Adopt form-based codes, which allow for the regulation of building form and placement rather than use.

- Revise parking ordinances to abolish parking minimums or to establish parking maximums.

- Build infill development by replacing underused parking lots with new residential, commercial, or mixed-use buildings located closer to the street.

To address car-oriented street design and operations:

- Adopt Complete Streets policies that commit to creating comprehensive networks to support walking, biking, and use of public transit.

- Change policies and practices that prioritize cars, revising project-selection criteria and establishing performance measures.

To overcome disincentives to private development:

- Adopt policies, such as annual registration fees, that penalize absentee property owners for leaving land vacant.

- Encourage investment with land-value tax policies.

- Offer small-scale loans and grants to help local business owners purchase the spaces they rent and improve their storefronts.

- Establish programs that provide training and support to aspiring business owners.

To overcome lack of local autonomy over roadways:

- Take local control of the speed, design, and operation of streets.

- Assume the costs of maintaining and operating state- or county-owned arterials at the city or town level.

- Encourage the state transportation department to adopt context-sensitive design guidance to give local governments more flexibility and autonomy.

- Create partnerships with business improvement districts and other community associations to introduce and maintain improvements to corridors.

Enhanced transit systems should include protected waiting areas with seating. (Rochester, Minnesota)

Above: A healthy corridor has improved infrastructure for pedestrians, bicyclists, and those with mobility challenges, such as people in wheelchairs. (Boise, Idaho)

Right: Commercial corridors have the potential to be vibrant places that reflect the culture of the surrounding community. (Columbus, Ohio)

From Unhealthy
to Healthy Corridors

Unhealthy corridors are everywhere, and they are deadly and costly for communities. As the audit research shows, primary arterials represent just 4 percent of the nation's total roadways but have accounted for almost 30 percent of traffic fatalities in recent years. Pedestrians and bicyclists are especially at risk, as are other vulnerable road users, including older people and Latinos. Low-income people who work along severely unhealthy corridors earn less than do members of the broader population.

Although the unhealthy conditions along commercial corridors can seem inevitable, in fact they are the result of specific policy and practice decisions about transportation priorities and land use patterns—decisions that can be changed over time in ways that improve health, safety, and economic development opportunities.

The Power of a Focus on Health

The corridor audit makes it clear that most urban and suburban arterials do not possess the attributes of a healthy corridor. So, how do communities get from the current state of affairs to something better?

A key insight from the past four years of the ULI Healthy Corridors project is that prioritizing health when reimagining problematic urban and suburban arterials can help align stakeholders and drive solutions. A focus on health can help ensure that the needs and well-being of the people who live, work, and travel along these streets are prioritized, and that the disparate impacts of policies and strategies on different groups of people are understood and addressed.

The social determinants of health take into account the fact that an individual or community's health is affected not just by genetics and access to high-quality health care, but also by the built and social environment—including housing conditions, transportation, education, and job opportunities.

How the emphasis on health plays out in planning corridor revitalization will vary place by place, but a focus on health can have profound implications for the allocation of resources and time. As an example, consensus among transportation and other state and local agencies about the importance of promoting health and protecting safety—rather than simply moving cars—can help ensure that strategies to improve the environment for pedestrians, bicyclists, and people with mobility challenges are part of transportation improvements. In addition, access to and across the corridor from adjacent neighborhoods can be enhanced in conjunction with corridor improvements.

Another example involves business development. Corridor improvement plans often call for redevelopment of underperforming retail spaces. An understanding of the social determinants of health, as well as a decision to prioritize the health of people currently living and working along corridors, can lead to introduction of complementary training and resources that help ensure that longtime small-business owners are able to remain and thrive as redevelopment occurs.

These examples illustrate how a focus on health can help inform priorities, approaches, and resource allocation. A holistic focus on health can help mobilize and energize community members, who have important insights and should play a critical role in any redevelopment planning. A focus on health can bring to the table new players from the public and private sectors, such as local health departments. And above all, a focus on health can help ensure that the needs and perspectives of the community are front and center.

Community stakeholders and residents should be engaged in corridor improvement discussions to ensure that changes reflect their needs.

Above: A healthy corridor has links to other parts of the community through well-connected street networks and transit options. (Cleveland, Ohio)

Right: Healthy corridors have well-marked and accessible crosswalks, a vibrant retail environment, and high-quality parks and public spaces. (Arlington, Virginia)

Arlington County

Understanding Healthy Corridors

The corridor audit used quantitative metrics to understand and measure corridor conditions. In that context, healthy corridors are defined as those that received the highest audit grades; they are pedestrian oriented, equitable, economically vibrant, and supportive of health and safety.

Our evolving understanding of health in the context of corridors builds on the qualitative and narrative definition that ULI developed over the course of the ULI Healthy Corridors Project and in collaboration with communities.

That definition, documented in the 2016 ULI publication *Building Healthy Corridors: Transforming Urban and Suburban Arterials into Thriving Places,* is:

A healthy corridor has land uses and services that allow residents and visitors to make healthy lifestyle choices more easily. A healthy corridor is a place that reflects the culture of the community, promotes social cohesion, inspires and facilitates healthy eating and active living, provides and connects to a variety of economic and educational opportunities and housing and transportation choices, and adapts to the needs and concerns of residents.

Figure 15: Attributes Shared by Healthy Corridors

Engaged and supported people who live, work, and travel along the corridor	• Engaged residents and local business owners • Organizations that facilitate long-term improvements and resident engagement • Regular programs in community gathering spaces • Accommodations for pets • Accommodations for vulnerable populations, including children, the elderly, and people with disabilities • A defined identity, drawing on the arts and culture of the community and supported by creative placemaking programming • Measures to address safety and perceptions of safety
Design and land use patterns that support community needs	• A vibrant retail environment • Housing options for all income levels • Buildings adjacent to or near sidewalks • Improved parking strategies and shared parking • High-quality parks and public spaces • Healthy food options
Improved infrastructure	• Plentiful, safe, and well-marked pedestrian crossings • Safe and well-marked bike lanes • Traffic speeds that accommodate pedestrians, bicyclists, and other users • Utility lines that are underground or blend into the surroundings • Sidewalks that link adjacent neighborhoods to the corridor and that are unobstructed, wide enough for a variety of users, and buffered from the street • Streetscapes that include amenities for visual interest and safety, including seating, trees for shade, and green buffers • Lighting that improves visibility and safety for pedestrians and bicyclists • Features that improve accessibility for all types of users, in compliance with Americans with Disabilities Act standards
Links to other parts of the city	• Well-connected, multimodal street networks • Safe and easily identifiable connections, including sidewalks and trails • Transit, including enhanced bus service or rail • Bike infrastructure on or adjacent to the corridor

Source: Urban Land Institute, *Building Healthy Corridors: Transforming Urban and Suburban Arterials into Thriving Places* (Washington, D.C.: Urban Land Institute, 2016).

BUILDING
Healthy Corridors
STRATEGY AND RESOURCE GUIDE

Nearly every community in the United States is plagued by underperforming commercial corridors. These arterials are characterized by wide roads, automobile-oriented services, buildings set back from the street, and narrow (or nonexistent) sidewalks. Residents who live along these corridors do not have easy access to healthy, fresh food; safe, walkable streets; and services that meet their everyday needs.

The design of these built environments have direct links to increases in chronic diseases such as Type 2 diabetes, asthma, and heart disease, all of which tend to be more prevalent in low-income communities and communities of color. However, by focusing on health as a core value for redevelopment, these corridors can be reshaped into places that put people—not cars and other vehicles—first.

It is important to note that the process of redeveloping these corridors into health-promoting places cannot—and should not—be done by only one type of stakeholder. A multitude of partners and stakeholders—including health professionals, planning and transportation departments, other city and county departments, the business community, real estate developers, architects and urban designers, and residents and community groups—must all be part of the process, from the beginning stages of communication and engagement to the later stage of setting the vision for the corridor and the final stage of implementation. Forming a corridor leadership group of a variety of stakeholders to oversee efforts, to plan workshops and convenings, and to help push decision making along helps ensure that the healthy corridor vision is ultimately implemented.

Building a healthier corridor means that health must be part of the process and the discussion from the very beginning. Many times political decision makers do not consider health when they implement new policies and programs or when they make built-environment-related decisions. By engaging health partners in planning decisions, a health perspective and health data can become a key part of decision-making processes. A specific tool to achieve this, the health impact assessment (HIA), can be used to analyze the impacts of a proposed policy, plan, or project on the health of current and future residents.

HIAs are typically led by health professionals, but planners, designers, developers, other stakeholders, and residents all have a role to play in the process to ensure that all perspectives are included and that the proposal minimizes negative health impacts and maximizes positive health benefits. However, an HIA is not required to bring a health perspective to land use changes; simply engaging with local health partners and ensuring that they are a key part of planning for corridor redevelopment can achieve this goal as well.

This guide provides a menu of strategies and resources for including a health focus within redevelopment efforts, and it is intended to serve as a resource for communities looking to redevelop commercial strip corridors. It complements the report *Building Healthy Corridors: Transforming Urban and Suburban Arterials into Thriving Places*, which can be downloaded from uli.org/healthycorridors.

A health impact assessment (HIA) is an evidence-based process that engages the community, gathers health-related information, and identifies strategies to improve community and individual health. Used to identify potential health impacts of projects, plans, and policies, HIAs consist of six phases typically used in other types of impact assessment: screening, scoping, assessment, recommendations, reporting, and evaluation and monitoring.

The "Building Healthy Corridors: Strategy and Resource Guide" provides approaches to help communities improve commercial corridors.

Healthy Corridor Audit Tool

How to Use:
» Complete the first section for the entire study area. Many indicators can be collected from existing data; they do not have to be collected on site.
» To assess the indicators in section 2, break the corridor into segments. The recommended assessment length is about 0.5 miles.
» Copy section 2 for subsequent segments.
» Take notes or include comments for subjective or qualitative ratings so that future assessors get an idea of why the rating was given.
» Take photos when possible, and include them with the audit for future reference.

Healthy Corridor Audit Tool: Baseline and Follow-up Conditions Assessment			
Corridor Name:		**Date Assessed:**	
		Field Notes	
Study area boundaries *(including blocks adjacent to corridor)*	North boundary:		
	South boundary:		
	East boundary:		
	West boundary:		
Length of corridor	Number of blocks:		
	Number of miles:		
General description *(neighborhoods encompassed, perceptions of area, etc.):*			

The "Healthy Corridor Audit Tool" helps communities track a variety of metrics during corridor improvement efforts.

ULI Resources for Healthier Corridors

Many communities are undertaking efforts to reimagine their commercial corridors and forge a path to a healthier future. There is no one-size-fits-all approach to this process. However, progress is possible if communities can come together to lay out a new vision and a plan for change. As demonstrated by the alternative approaches described earlier in this report, there are many tools in the policy and practice toolbox.

ULI's comprehensive "Building Healthy Corridors: Strategy and Resource Guide," is a resource for communities looking for ways to move forward on overhauling problematic corridors and for specific partners and professionals seeking to engage in this effort. The guide offers specific recommendations on and resources for engaging the community and agreeing on a vision, using programming and existing community assets to inspire change, overhauling automobile-oriented transportation infrastructure, and financing redevelopment projects on and adjacent to the street.

The guide is organized into four categories:

- **Community Engagement and Visioning Strategies.** This section covers determining which stakeholders from a variety of groups and sectors should be engaged, and how to engage them; tactics for authentic resident engagement; identification of the corridor's assets and challenges; and using lessons from these processes to craft a vision for the corridor and adjacent neighborhoods.

- **Design, Arts, Culture, and Programming.** This section explores leveraging the assets and opportunities identified as part of the corridor visioning process through specific tactics, programs, and opportunities to create a new identity or enhance an existing identity for the neighborhood.

- **Infrastructure Overhaul.** This section describes the types of infrastructure needed to support all users; strategies for and examples of zoning codes for healthier infrastructure and land uses; and policies that can help stakeholders evaluate corridor changes and performance.

- **Who Pays? Financing and Policy for Equitable and Inclusive Redevelopment.** This section addresses ways to finance improvements, which should be investigated at the outset of a corridor redevelopment process. It presents a variety of financing strategies, including user fee–based financing, development transaction–based financing, transportation-based financing, and a menu of grants and loans from the public sector.

An additional resource is ULI's "Healthy Corridor Audit Tool," which helps communities measure baseline conditions along the corridor and the adjacent neighborhoods. The tool looks at 60 indicators to help stakeholders understand current corridor conditions. The audit includes indicators to measure residential property conditions, general amenities and land uses, types and the condition of businesses and institutions, transportation and road conditions, services along the corridor, and physical characteristics.

Analysis of audit data can help communities identify challenges and opportunities, determine where to focus initial efforts, and measure and track changes over time in order to ensure that changes remain positive for current and future residents and business owners.

ULI recommends that this audit be conducted in order to understand conditions before corridor improvement efforts are carried out, and that conditions be reassessed at regular intervals once improvements have been made.

Both the strategy and resource guide and the audit tool are available for download at **uli.org/healthycorridors**.

Change Is Possible

It will take a coalition of stakeholders to bring about positive change along America's dangerous and underperforming urban and suburban arterials. In many ways, they are among the country's forgotten places—often ugly, unloved, unsafe, and neglected. Unhealthy corridors are the country's collective blind spots.

But if the right mix of strategies can be brought to bear on them, they are also places with vast potential. Corridors can be vibrant and vital main streets, community focal points, a home to businesses, restaurants, jobs, and housing. They can play host to public art and offer places for people to meet, to linger, to mix with one another. They can be multimodal and safer for people of all backgrounds and abilities. Unhealthy corridors should not be left as they are, to continue jeopardizing the health and well-being of the people who live and work along them. Healthier corridors are possible. **What are we waiting for?**

Notes

1. *Building Healthy Corridors: Transforming Urban and Suburban Arterials into Thriving Places,* the 2016 ULI report that resulted from the two-year Healthy Corridors project, is available at uli.org/wp-content/uploads/ULI-Documents/Building-Healthy-Corridors-ULI.pdf.

2. National Highway Traffic Safety Administration (NHTSA), "Fatality Analysis Reporting System (FARS) Encyclopedia," 2018, www-fars.nhtsa.dot.gov/Main/index.aspx; Federal Highway Administration, "Highway Statistics 2014," 2014, www.fhwa.dot.gov/policyinformation/statistics/2014/hm220.cfm.

3. Smart Growth America, *Measuring Sprawl 2014,* 2014, https://smartgrowthamerica.org/resources/measuring-sprawl-2014.

4. ULI and SGA analysis of NHTSA's FARS data.

5. ULI and SGA analysis of NHTSA's FARS data.

6. The Form-Based Codes Institute has gathered the best examples of form-based codes in "Library of Codes," available at https://formbasedcodes.org/codes.

7. City of Haltom City, Haltom City Zoning Map, www.haltomcitytx.com/maps-planning-community-development/haltom-city-zoning-map.

8. City of Haltom City, "Code of Ordinances," https://library.municode.com/tx/haltom_city/codes/code_of_ordinances.

9. National Complete Streets Coalition, "Complete Streets policies nationwide," 2018, https://smartgrowthamerica.org/program/national-complete-streets-coalition/publications/policy-development/policy-atlas.

10. WATE-TV staff, "Pedestrian Killed by Car on Clinton Highway," December 24, 2017, www.wate.com/news/local-news/pedestrian-killed-by-car-on-clinton-highway/881195368.

11. Wallace E. Oates and Robert M. Schwab, "The Impact of Urban Land Taxation: The Pittsburgh Experience," *National Tax Journal* 50, no.1 (1997): 1–21.

12. City of Gary and the Harris School of Public Policy, University of Chicago, "Gary Counts," 2016, http://garycounts.org.

13. Erin Devorah Rapoport, "The Politics of Disinvestment and Development in Gary, Indiana," *Advocates' Forum,* 2014, www.ssa.uchicago.edu/politics-disinvestment-and-development-gary-indiana; Carole Carlson, "IRS Forgives Most of Gary Schools' $8.4 Million Tax Problem, Freeing Vacant Schools for Sale," *Chicago Tribune,* April 11, 2018, www.chicagotribune.com/suburbs/post-tribune/news/ct-ptb-gary-irs-lien-st-0412-story.html.

14. Northwest Indiana Regional Development Authority, "Northwest Indiana RDA," 2018, www.rdatransformation.com; Chris Bentley, "How Gary, Indiana, Got Serious about Tackling Blight," *CityLab,* February 26, 2015, www.citylab.com/equity/2015/02/how-gary-indiana-got-serious-about-tackling-blight/386159.

15. Urban Land Institute, *Building Healthy Corridors: Transforming Urban and Suburban Arterials into Thriving Places* (Washington, D.C.: Urban Land Institute, 2016), 20–21, uli.org/wp-content/uploads/ULI-Documents/Edgewater-Drive-Orlando-FL.pdf.

16. Tennessee Department of Transportation, *Multimodal Project Scoping Manual,* 2018, www.tn.gov/content/dam/tn/tdot/multimodaltransportation/TDOT%20Multimodal%20Project%20Scoping%20Manual.pdf.

17. Patrick McGeehan, "Christie Outlines a Plan to Pay for Transit Work," *New York Times,* January 6, 2011, www.nytimes.com/2011/01/07/nyregion/07christie.html.

18. Somerset County, *Making Connections: Somerset County's Circulation Plan Update,* November 2011, www.co.somerset.nj.us/home/showdocument?id=15618.

19. David Matthau, 2017, "Route 206 bypass still a $45M road to nowhere—but work resuming soon," *New Jersey 101.5* (WXKM-FM website), August 16, 2017, http://nj1015.com/route-206-bypass-still-a-45m-road-to-nowhere-but-work-resuming-soon.

20. New Jersey Department of Transportation, "Route 206 Hillsborough Bypass Final Construction Begins," April 13, 2018, www.nj.gov/transportation/about/press/2018/041318.shtm.

Acknowledgments

ULI and SGA gratefully acknowledge the contributions of participants in a workshop held at the Intersections: Creating Culturally Complete Streets conference in Nashville in April 2018, as well as the following people:

Karen Adelman
Senior Communications Strategist
Metropolitan Area Planning Council

Tim Anderson
Principal
META Landscape Architecture

Alex Carmack
Programs Manager
Alzheimer's Association

Ed Christopher
Transportation Consultant

Patti Clare
Senior Planner
Neel-Shaffer Inc.

Anthony Corso
Chief Innovation Officer
City of Peoria, Illinois

Sara Cox
Healthy Development Coordinator
Tennessee Department of Health

Charles Drayton
City Planner
City of North Charleston,
 South Carolina

Dan Eernissee
Economic Development Director
City of Everett, Washington

Peter Friedrichs
Director of Innovative Initiatives
The Policastro Group

Calvin Gladney
President and Chief Executive Officer
Smart Growth America

Juanita Hardy
Senior Visiting Fellow for
 Creative Placemaking
Urban Land Institute

Kurt Heischmidt
Healthy Development Coordinator
Tennessee Department of Health

Chris Kochtitzky
Senior Adviser
Physical Activity and Health Program
U.S. Centers for Disease Control
 and Prevention

Margaret Kubilins
Traffic Engineering Manager
VHB

Stuart Levin
Physician, Wake Internal Medicine Consultants
President, Blue Ridge Corridor Alliance

Sheila Lynch
Land Use Program Supervisor
Tri-County Health Department

Bert Mathews
President
The Mathews Company

Gretchen Milliken
Director, Advanced Planning
Louisville (Kentucky) Metro Government

Jessica Nguyen
Planner
ChangeLab Solutions

Paxton Roberts
Executive Director
Bike NWA

Sharon Roerty
Senior Program Officer
Robert Wood Johnson Foundation

Anwar Saleem
Executive Director
H Street Main Street Inc.

Mark VanderSchaaf
Placemaking Consultant
Forecast Public Art

John Vick
Evaluation and Assessment Director
Office of Primary Prevention
Tennessee Department of Health

Jamie Rae Walker
Associate Professor and Extension
 Specialist
Texas A&M University
Agrilife Extension

Kathryn Wehr
Senior Program Officer
Robert Wood Johnson Foundation

Clark Wilson
Acting Director
Community Assistance and Research Division
U.S. Environmental Protection Agency

Derrick Lanardo Woody
Chief Executive Officer
DLW LLC